**Fife** COUNCIL

Fife Council Education Department

King's Road Primary School

King's Crescent, Rosyth KY11 2RS

# *Food*

# EGGS

## Louise Spilsbury

Heinemann
LIBRARY

**H** www.heinemann.co.uk/library
Visit our website to find out more information about Heinemann Library books.

To order:
☎ Phone 44 (0) 1865 888066
📄 Send a fax to 44 (0) 1865 314091
💻 Visit the Heinemann Bookshop at www.heinemann.co.uk/library to browse our catalogue and order online.

First published in Great Britain by Heinemann Library,
Halley Court, Jordan Hill, Oxford OX2 8EJ
a division of Reed Educational and Professional Publishing Ltd.
Heinemann is a registered trademark of Reed Educational & Professional Publishing Ltd.

OXFORD MELBOURNE AUCKLAND
JOHANNESBURG BLANTYRE GABORONE
IBADAN PORTSMOUTH (NH) USA CHICAGO

Designed by Celia Floyd
Illustrated by Barry Atkinson
Originated by Ambassador Litho Ltd
Printed by South China Printing Co in Hong Kong.

ISBN 0 431 12702 6
05 04 03 02 01
10 9 8 7 6 5 4 3 2 1

**British Library Cataloguing in Publication Data**
Spilsbury, Louise
    Eggs. – (Food)
    1. Eggs  2. Cookery (Eggs)
    I. Title
    641.3'75

**Acknowledgements**
The Publishers would like to thank the following for permission to reproduce photographs:
Anthony Blake Photo Library p.10; Gareth Boden pp.6, 11, 22, 23, 25, 28, 29; Bruce Coleman Ltd/Jane Burton p.15; Corbis pp.12, /James L Amos p.9, /Anthony Bannister/Gallo Images p.8, /Ed Eckstein p.18, /Layne Kennedy p.20, /George Lepp p.21, /Chris Mattison/Frank Lane Agency p.7; Holt Studios/Nigel Cattlin p.17; Photodisc p.5; SPL/Hugh Turvey p.4; Tony Stone pp.13, /Mitch Kezar p.19, /Dennis O'Clair p.24, /Tony Page p.16.

Cover photograph reproduced with permission of Gareth Boden.

Every effort has been made to contact copyright holders of any material reproduced in this book. Any omissions will be rectified in subsequent printings if notice is given to the Publisher.

# CONTENTS

Words written in bold, **like this**, are explained in the Glossary.

# WHAT ARE EGGS?

All **female** birds **lay** eggs. Some of these eggs are **fertilized**. That means a **chick** is growing inside them.

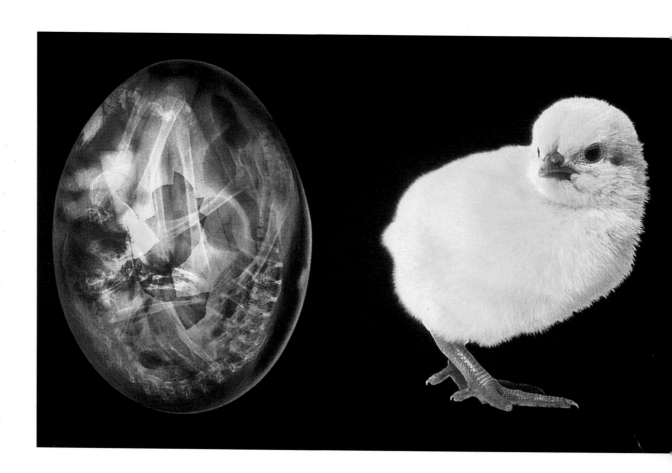

Eggs are a useful food for people. The eggs we eat are not fertilized. They do not have chicks growing inside.

# KINDS OF EGGS

Most people eat **hens'** eggs. You can eat other eggs too, like duck or **quail**. Ducks' eggs are bigger than hens' eggs. Quails lay small, speckled eggs.

duck's egg          hen's egg          quail's egg

Other animals **lay** eggs too, including
**reptiles** and fish. This Baird's rat
snake has laid three eggs. They have
soft **shells**.

# IN THE PAST

Long ago, people took eggs from the **nests** of wild birds to eat. Some people still eat wild bird eggs today. This **nomad** in Africa has found **ostrich** eggs to eat.

People began to keep birds so they could eat the eggs when they wanted. Today some families keep a few chickens so they can eat fresh eggs.

# AROUND THE WORLD

People all over the world eat eggs. In Spain people use eggs and vegetables to make one of their favourite dishes – a Spanish omelette.

China **produces** more eggs than any other country in the world. Chinese people eat eggs in lots of different ways. This is Chinese egg fried rice.

# LAYING EGGS

In the wild, birds build **nests** to **lay** their eggs in. Nests are often made of twigs, with a soft layer of grass or feathers for the eggs to rest on.

Birds sit on their eggs to keep them warm. The warmth helps the **chicks** inside grow. Parent birds may take turns sitting on the nest.

# INSIDE AN EGG

When a **chick** begins to grow inside an egg it is called an **embryo**. The **shell** protects it. The **yolk** is food to help the chick grow. The **white** keeps it moist.

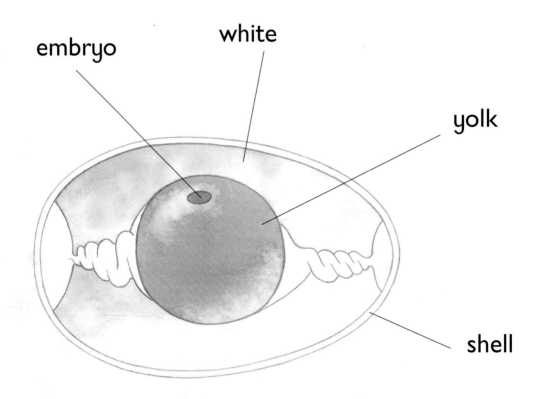

embryo

white

yolk

shell

Chicks take between 11 and 80 days to grow inside their egg. When the chick is big enough, it breaks out of the egg.

# EGGS WE EAT

Many of the eggs we eat are **free range**. This means that they come from farms where **hens** wander freely all day. At night the hens go into a hen house.

Boxes line the sides of the hen house. Hens **lay** their eggs in the boxes. The eggs roll onto an outside shelf. The farmer collects them from there.

# BIG FARMS

Most of the eggs we buy come from big **hen** farms. Here, hens stay in rows of small cages all the time.

The eggs the hens **lay** roll onto a **conveyor belt**. Workers remove any cracked or dirty eggs as they move along. The rest go into large trays.

# EGGS TO YOU

The trays of eggs are taken to a
packing station. Here a machine
weighs the eggs, and then sorts
them into sizes.

The eggs are packed into boxes.
These hold the eggs safely. Each box
or egg has the date marked on it. This
tells **consumers** how fresh they are.

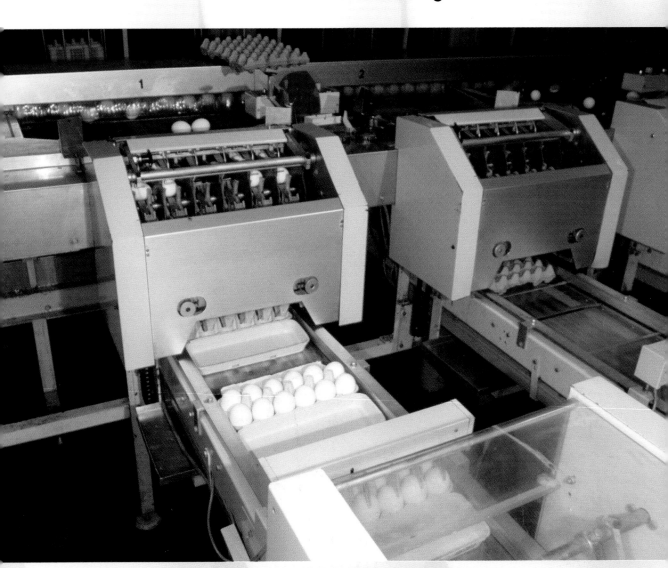

# EATING EGGS

Cooking eggs in different ways makes them look and taste different. You can boil eggs with their **shells** on, scramble them in a pan or fry them in butter or oil.

boiled egg

fried egg

scrambled egg

You can use eggs to make pancakes.
You can mix them with other foods
such as flour, sugar and margarine, to
make cakes. You can **whisk** egg
**whites** to make meringues.

# GOOD FOR YOU

Eggs are a useful food. They contain **protein** and **vitamins**. These **nutrients** help you grow and keep you healthy.

Eggs are good for you, although you should not eat too many. When you eat them it is best to cook them well first. Uncooked eggs can make you ill.

# HEALTHY EATING

You need to eat different kinds of food to keep well. This food pyramid shows how much of each different food you need.

The foods in the group at the bottom of the pyramid can be eaten at every meal. You should eat some of the foods shown in the middle groups every day.

Eggs are in the middle. You need only small amounts of the foods at the top.

The food in each part of the pyramid helps your body in different ways.

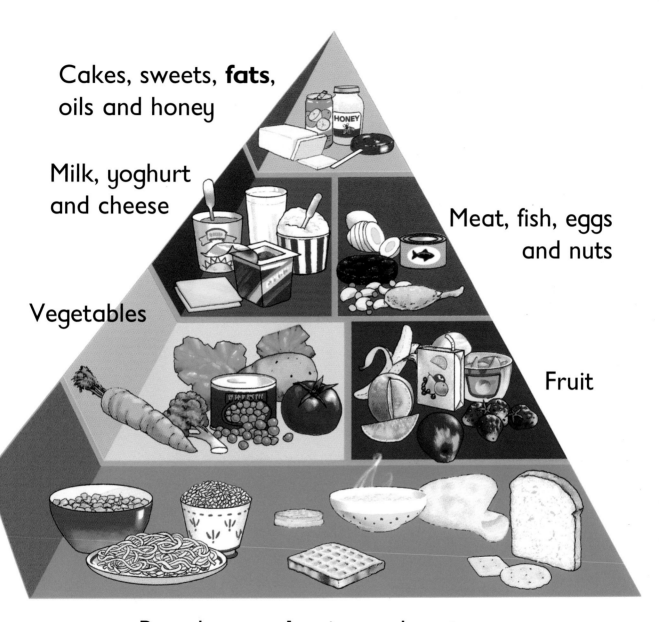

Cakes, sweets, **fats**, oils and honey

Milk, yoghurt and cheese

Meat, fish, eggs and nuts

Vegetables

Fruit

Bread, **cereals**, rice and pasta

# SCRAMBLED EGGS RECIPE

1 Crack the eggs into a bowl. Add the milk.

2 Mix the eggs and milk with a fork or **whisk**.

**You will need:**
- 2 eggs
- 2 tablespoons of milk
- 1 teaspoon of butter, or oil

whisk

Ask an adult to help you!

28

3 Melt the butter or oil in a pan. When it sizzles, add the eggs.

4 Cook over a low heat, stirring all the time. They should look like this when ready.

# GLOSSARY

**cereals** grains like wheat and rice that are used to make flour, bread and breakfast foods

**chick** baby bird

**consumers** people who buy things that they need or want, such as food

**conveyor belt** endless moving tray that carries things along

**embryo** unborn or unhatched baby

**fat** nutrient found in some foods. Butter, oil and margarine are kinds of fat.

**female** girl or woman. Female animals can give birth to young animals like themselves.

**fertilized** when an egg is able to grow into a baby that will look like its parent

**free range** chicken that is allowed to wander freely all day

**hen** female chicken

**lay** when an egg comes out of a female bird's body

**nest** made by birds to lay their eggs in. Nests may be made from twigs, grass and mud.

**nomad**   person who moves around instead of always living in one place

**nutrients**   goodness in food that helps us stay healthy

**ostrich**   largest bird in the world. It cannot fly but it runs very fast.

**produce**   when a country or person grows or makes things that people want to buy, like food

**protein**   nutrient needed to help our bodies grow and repair themselves

**quail**   small bird with short tail feathers. People sometimes keep quails for their eggs.

**reptiles**   group of animals that includes snakes, tortoises and lizards. Most reptiles lay eggs.

**shell**   covering around an egg that keeps the inside safe

**vitamins**   group of nutrients needed to keep your body well and help you grow

**whisk**   stir quickly with a kitchen tool called a whisk

**white**   the white part inside an egg

**yolk**   the yellow part inside an egg. If a chick is growing inside an egg, it uses the yolk as f

# MORE BOOKS TO READ

*Farm Animals: Chickens*, Rachael Bell,
    Heinemann Library, 2000
*Life Cycle of a Chicken*, Angela Royston,
    Heinemann Library, 1998
*Safe and Sound: Eat Well*, Angela Royston,
    Heinemann Library, 1999
*What's for Lunch? Eggs*, Franklin Watts
*Breakfast Around the World*, Franklin Watts

# INDEX

# Titles in the *Food* series include:

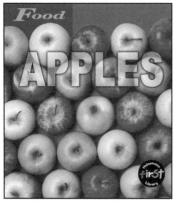

Hardback    0 431 12708 5

Hardback    0 431 12700 X

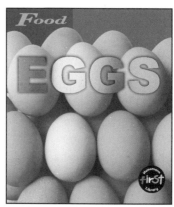

Hardback    0 431 12702 6

Hardback    0 431 12706 9

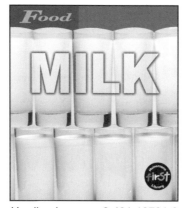

Hardback    0 431 12701 8

Hardback    0 431 12703 4

Hardback    0 431 12707 7

Hardback    0 431 12705 0

Find out about the other titles in this series on our website www.heinemann.co.uk/library